LET'S START
STILLWATER
CARP
FISHING

Richard Willett

The Crowood Press

First published in 1990 by
The Crowood Press
Ramsbury, Marlborough,
Wiltshire SN8 2HE

British Library Cataloguing in Publication Data

Willett, Richard
    Stillwater carp fishing.
    1. Carp. Angling. Manuals
    I. Title
    799.1'752

    ISBN 1-85223-308-7

Typeset by Jahweh Associates, Stroud
Printed in Great Britain by MacLehose & Partners Ltd

Contents

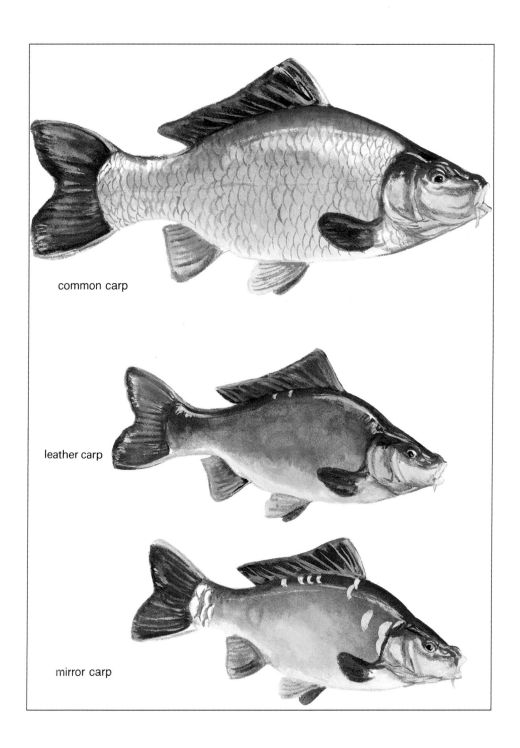

common carp

leather carp

mirror carp

4

Carp

This is a species that dwells in stillwaters of all kinds – lakes, ponds and gravel pits. Carp are large, heavily built fish that will grow very big in favourable conditions. Most waters are stocked with fish that have been reared in fish farms.

There are three varieties of carp: the common, the most handsome, being fully scaled and a beautiful golden-bronze colour; the mirror, a fish that has a number of large scales generally found along the lateral line; and the leather variety which has a total absence of scaling.

There are also two distinct types of common carp: the huge deep-bodied type that has been introduced to many stillwaters from stock-bred fish on the Continent and a slimmer, more slightly built fish called the 'wildie' which is thought to be derived from the original fish brought to Britain by ecclesiastics in the Middle Ages. Carp in the right kind of habitat can grow in excess of fifty pounds.

The carp has four barbules – two protuberances from above the upper jaw and one at each corner of the mouth. There are no teeth in the jaws but teeth are present on the pharyngeal bones. Carp prefer a soft muddy bottom in which they find much of their food and into which they can sink to lie during the winter months. As the year warms, carp begin to rise in the water seeking food, usually in the form of minute invertebrates. During the summer months they normally spend their time very close to the surface.

Location

Locating carp in a lake or pond is not very difficult. In the hot weather they will frequently bask just below the surface. They will also show signs of themselves by rolling, making a great disturbance to the water's surface. When they are feeding on the lake bed they will disturb lots of silt and discolour the water. If the lake or pond bed is soft, groups of bubbles will rise to the surface, often accompanied by bits of weed and twigs.

The most difficult type of water in which to locate carp is a vast gravel pit. Location on this type of water is often done by trial and error.

fishing position

reed bed – an ideal place to put a floating bait

tree providing shady area – a bait could be placed among the lilies here

open water – carp will

reed bed – float fish
or free-line a bait

d

lilies – hold large carp

fishing position

Free-Lining

Free-lining, as the name suggests, is simply a method of presenting the fish with a baited hook on the end of a line using no additional weight. The bait has to be large enough to cast without weight. Bites are easy to detect by watching the point where the line enters the water. As a fish picks up the bait the line will start twitching and then the bow in the line between the rod and the water will begin to lift and tighten.

Free-lining a large bait to catch carp is a deadly method. The classic example of this is to use a piece of floating crust. The crust is fastened onto the hook and cast out onto the surface of the lake. This is a very exciting method of fishing, especially when a large carp comes slowly circling around your bait. It is tempting to strike too soon when you actually see the carp open its mouth and suck in the bread crust. Control the strike until the fish turns and your line pulls across the surface.

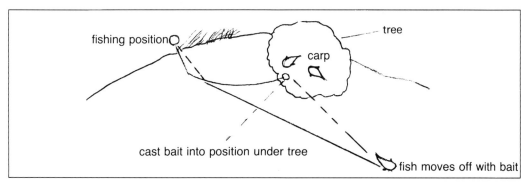

fishing position ⃝   tree

carp

cast bait into position under tree

fish moves off with bait

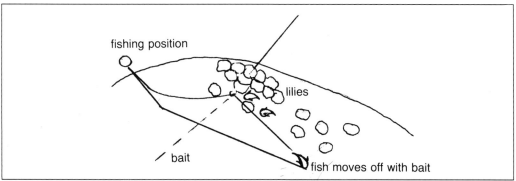

fishing position ⃝

lilies

bait

fish moves off with bait

Legering

The tackle needed for catching carp must be strong, especially if the water you are fishing is full of lily beds and thick weeds. The rod should be 10 or 11 feet in length. Even small carp in open water fight well so your line strength should be of at least 5-pound breaking strain. On really weedy waters where the carp grow large, a breaking strain of 12 pounds is not too heavy. The type of rod to handle this breaking strain of line should be a carp rod of about 11 foot in length with a test curve of about 2 pounds.

When fishing a bait at long range for carp it is easier to cast further using leger tackle. Most carp waters contain a lot of small fish such as rudd and roach so the bait should be chosen and presented in a way that will deter these fish. Sweetcorn or meat baits have proved to be good carp baits. Scatter a few samples on the lake bed and then present a sample on a size 8 hook in the centre of these. Do not delay the strike as carp will pick these up quickly.

Leger terminal tackle should be kept as basic as possible – *see* the rigs illustrated. When finicky carp are proving difficult to hook, a bolt rig is the answer. The fish picks up the bait and feels the resistance from a non free-running lead, thus feeling the hook; it will bolt off with the bait, making a very positive run.

If large paste baits are used, carp are more likely to pick up a bait and run with it. Whilst legering with large baits the rod should be mounted on two rod rests. The front rest should be the type which has deep groove in it to allow the line to run freely and not become trapped under the rod, and set lower than the back one so that the rod is inclined towards the water. In really windy weather the rod tip should be submerged to cut out wind interference on the line.

When using large baits, the bail arm on the reel should be left open so that the fish can take line without feeling any resistance. As the fish begins to run with the bait, lift the rod, close the bail arm and strike as the line tightens up. Bites can be detected by folding a piece of silver paper over the line. This will fall clear when you strike into the fish. When legering small baits, however, the bail arm should be closed and some form of bobbin indicator fastened on the line between the first two rod rings. Carp which pick up the bait and don't move very far cause the bobbin to jerk up and down rapidly. Thise are often referred to as 'twitchers'.

Anglers who specialise in carp fishing have devised many complicated and ingenious methods for detecting bites and for terminal rigs. The beginner will catch plenty of carp and still get the same pleasure out of carp fishing without some of these refinements.

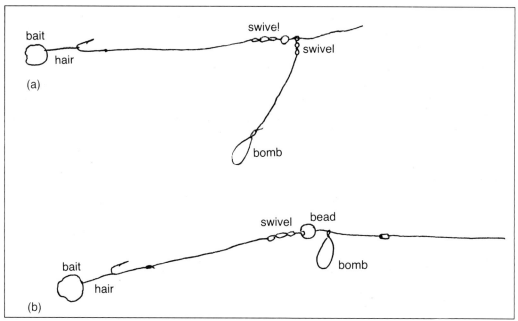

(a)   Basic leger rig.   (b)   Bolt rig.

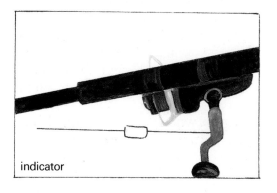

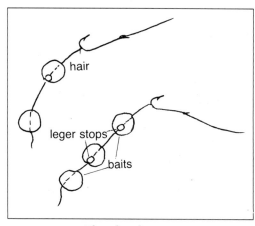

Three-bait hair rig.

Float Fishing

In recent years a lot of mystique has grown around carp fishing. Some of it can be justified, in that many carp in hard-fished waters are difficult to catch. However, enjoyable fishing for carp is still available. One of the most exciting methods of fishing for carp, under the right circumstances, is float fishing.

Carp will feed amongst the underwater stems of reed-mace and bulrush where they eat snails' eggs and small nymphs clinging to the stalks. As the large fish move amongst the stems of the rushes, they cause the tops to move frantically. When carp are feeding like this a float-fished bait up against these stems will almost always produce fish. Your tackle will need to be strong to cope with snags and guard against breakages amongst weed like this. A rod of about 1¼ pounds' test curve will suffice; a line of about 7-pound breaking strain will also be needed. Gaps in weed beds and lily beds will also produce carp.

Not all float rigs are designed for minimum resistance; some of them are out-and-out shock rigs. But all of them have one thing in common: instant bite signalling that allows for a quick response from the angler. Any movement of the float will almost always be from fish feeding either close to, or on the bait, or very close to the float. Keep a good hold on the rod as bites my be frantic. Once you have hooked a carp try to steer it away from the lilies and into snag-free water. Take your time if necessary and be patient – it will be worth it.

A good method (with flat float) where carp might move in very close to the margins and could give you line bites on any other methods of presentation.

1. Float fishing in fairly clear, very shallow swims just out from the marginal growth.
2. Float set well over depth.
3. Baits should be large paste bait, meat, worms or bread.

When carp give you this kind of action you've got it made. A carp hooked on light float tackle.

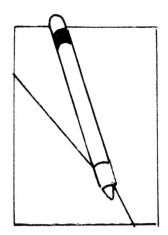

The lift method. A length of peacock quill fastened bottom-only with a float rubber.

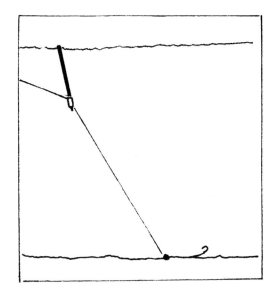

Baits

Anticipation is part of the enjoyment of fishing, and the preparation of baits for a day's fishing greatly enhances this anticipation. Some baits can be bought from your local tackle shop whilst others have to be collected.

Maggot Without doubt, the most convenient and most widely used bait is the maggot. More than one type of maggot can be bought commercially. The main one used is the larvae of the blow fly: this is used as hookbait. Pinkies and squatts are small so are used as loose feed. Another type is the gozzer which is a good hookbait for bream. To keep maggots at their best, store them in a cool dry place.

Caster The next stage of the metamorphosis of the maggot before it turns into a fly. They are ideal as a loose feed bait and are often mixed with groundbait. They are also a good hookbait and will produce better-quality fish.

Lobworm A very good big-fish bait. Take a torch out on a warm evening and walk out onto the lawn. If the ground is moist you will see them lying on the grass. If you are quite stealthy you should be able to fill a bait box quickly. They are best kept in damp moss.

Redworm   A very lively worm.

Bread   A loaf of bread can provide three excellent baits for fishing.

Bread crust   A very good bait. It can be used floating on the surface, resting on a submerged weed bed or floating just off the bottom. A bait favoured by many big fish hunters and an excellent carp bait.

Bread paste   Using clean hands, a paste is made by mixing the centre of the loaf with water. Place the mixture in a clean towel and remove any excess moisture. Then knead it until the right consistency is reached. The paste can also be flavoured and coloured during this process. Two good additives are cheese and custard powder.

Bread flake   Fresh bread is best suited for this. Pinch out a piece of bread from the middle of the loaf. Squeeze part of it onto the rear end of the hook shank and leave the bread which covers the bend of the hook in its natural state.

Cheese   A favourite bait with many anglers as there are so many different sorts. A good bait for many coarse fish.

Sweetcorn   A very good bait for carp. An expensive bait but well worth using.

Luncheon meat A great bait for carp, either float fished or on leger. Please open the tin at home and leave it there, not on the bank side.

Potato Tinned potatoes are a good choice to start with. A very good carp bait.

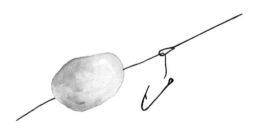

Hempseed On a water which is regularly fished with hemp, this is a deadly bait from the start. It is also a very good bait to use as loose feed or mixed in your groundbait. The seed has to be cooked until it splits before it can be used. Ready-cooked hemp can now be bought and this is just as good.

Tares Larger than hemp and needs a little more cooking. Used in conjunction with hemp it is a deadly combination.

Groundbait This is a mixture that is introduced into the swim you are fishing, or into a swim days before you fish it (this is called 'pre-baiting'). Brown breadcrumbs make a good base, mixed with water. It should have the consistency which allows it to be shaped into balls the size of golf balls. It should not crumble. Samples of baits can be added to the groundbait base: maggots, casters, hemp or sweetcorn can be added, for example.

These balls are introduced by hand or with the aid of a catapult into the swim where they disintegrate. Heavy groundbaiting can often do more harm than good. Little and often is a more sensible policy.

Knots

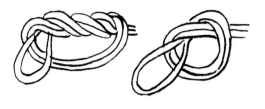 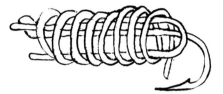

Three-turn Loop knot.

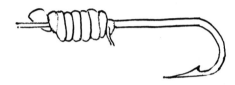

Spade End knot.

Method of joining hook length to reel line.

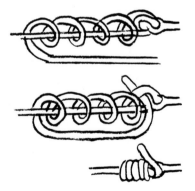

Clinch knot.

Playing and Landing

On hooking a fish, especially a large one, keep the tip of the rod well up and maintain a steady pressure. Never point the rod at the fish. The clutch on the reel must be adjusted prior to fishing so that it yields line when the pressure on it is just below the breaking strain of the line.

If a hooked fish makes for an area where underwater snags exist, it can be turned by applying side-strain.

Have the net close at hand. When the fish shows signs of tiring, slip the net into the water and keep it stationary.

Never jab at the fish in an attempt to scoop it out. Bring the fish over the awaiting net, not the net to the fish.

Handling and Hook Removal

Always make sure your hands are wet before handling fish. Grip the fish firmly but gently just behind the gill covers.

If the hook is lightly embedded near the front of the mouth, it is possible to remove it with the fingertips; otherwise, use a disgorger.

With larger fish, it is best to leave them lying in the damp net while you remove the hook. Artery forceps are best for this. When they are locked, a really good grip is maintained on the hook, which can be gently eased out. A damp towel positioned between the hand and the fish is advisable, as carp are very strong and need some holding if they suddenly decide to leap about.

Retaining and Returning Fish

Fish should be retained only in a large knotless keepnet, which is well covered by water, preferably in a shaded area. Never keep them for any length of time; in fact, there is no point in retaining them at all unless they are to be weighed or photographed at the end of your fishing session. Carp are best retained in keepsacks where they will lie quietly.

Never throw a fish into a net, but place it in gently, using wet hands.

When returning fish, gently gather up the net until the area occupied by the fish is reached; place the mouth of the net underwater and allow the fish to swim off.

A carp should be held underwater in an upright position with both hands until it swims away.

Index